Workplace Bullying

A 5-Step Guide to Overcoming a Hostile Work Environment

by Noah Sullivan

Table of Contents

Introduction

40 hours a week, 173 hours a month, 2080 hours a year. No matter how you slice it, it's just too much time to spend in a hostile work environment. Being the victim of bullying at work is detrimental to your workplace satisfaction and productivity, not to mention your personal health. Good companies do not tolerate bullying, and for good reason.

Bullying at work can take many forms. Before you even begin to take the proper steps to overcoming a hostile work environment, it's important that you learn to call a spade a spade. If you're being regularly shouted at or diminished, especially in front of customers or colleagues, you're probably being bullied. If you're on the receiving end of snide and degrading comments, you're probably being bullied. If you're being gossiped about, overloaded with work, or purposefully excluded or made to feel unwelcome, then you're probably being bullied. Workplace bullying can take many forms, but odds are, you'll know it when you see it, and you'll definitely know it when you experience it.

In order for this book to help you take the steps to address workplace bullying, you must first be willing to acknowledge the fact that you're being bullied. It may be tempting to try and rationalize the behavior of a supervisor or co-worker, attributing their behavior to "just being a part of their personality," or worse, buying into the fallacy that you somehow deserve to be treated with disrespect and cruelty. Adopting these views will only ensure that the bullying you're experiencing continues. It may even become worse. You owe it to yourself, for health reasons alone, to take action to remedy the situation. The 5 steps outlined and detailed in this book are going to help you do exactly that. Let's get started to put an end to this ASAP.

Step 1: Sizing Up the Situation

Assess How Bullying Impacts Your Health and Work Performance

You owe it to yourself to know what's truly at stake if you allow yourself to remain in a hostile work environment. Enduring stress and harassment can eat away at your psyche, especially when you're enduring it for several hours of almost every day. Even if you don't work directly with your bully for most of the work day, simply being in an environment where you've always got the specter of harassment, degradation, and personal conflict hanging over your head can take a huge toll on your wellbeing.

To help you identify the personal ramifications of your hostile work environment, take note of the following signs:

a.) You're not sleeping well. You struggle to sleep through the night. You wake up full of dread, in glum anticipation of another day in your hostile work environment;

b.) You find yourself feeling nauseous before or during work. You may even vomit without cause. This may be the result of the anxiety you feel about your workplace;

c.) You begin to entertain guilt feelings surrounding your work life. You begin to beat yourself up for provoking the bullying behavior. Or you beat yourself up because you know that what's happening to you at work is not ok, but you don't feel as if you've the power to do anything about it;

d.) Your friends or family begin to notice how frequently you complain about your workplace and the people in it;

e.) Your enjoyment of weekends or holidays is tainted by fear and anxiety about your imminent return to work;

f.) Your physician notices new problems with your general health. Your blood pressure has gone up or you're suddenly losing your hair or feeling regularly depressed. Maybe you're losing or gaining weight, or you've abandoned an exercise regimen or diet.

When you weigh the full range of the ramifications from workplace bullying, you get to take a sober, realistic look at the gravity of the situation. You will understand and accept that what's happening at work cannot continue. You will accept that this is a severe matter that warrants your attention, and you will resolve to undertake a plan of remedial action, even if it means leaving your job.

Take Control and Respond Proactively

A lot of individuals may have a very difficult time looking their bullying problem square in the eye and accepting its severity. What if you don't think you could possibly find another job? You've got bills to pay, a family to support. If you insist that your current job is vital, then you're already going to be at a disadvantage. You'll be more inclined to endure poor treatment at work, especially if your supervisor is the culprit. If this is you, don't worry. We're going to need to spend some time adjusting your outlook. Here's how you reposition yourself to a more powerful footing:

a) Take some time off. If you happen to have some personal or sick days at the ready, or a flexible vacation week, use it. Taking a nice stretch of off-time will let you reacquaint yourself with the person you are outside of work. If you can, get out of town for a while. Go see Niagara Falls or Mount Rushmore. You need to remind yourself the reality of the big wide world that lies beyond the confines of your workplace. Even a short time away should leave you feeling more optimistic about what's possible for your life, should you be unsuccessful at permanently ending the bullying you're experiencing at work. Because, the fact is, you will either be successful or leave your job. You're not going to commit yourself to indefinite ongoing abuse;

b) Focus on your personal wellness outside of work. What happens in the movies when someone is getting beat up or bullied? They go learn judo or boxing, and the next time they're harassed they serve up a nice pop in the nose. Everyone lives happily ever after. Maybe you're not going to be blacking any eyes in the office, but it doesn't mean that this isn't a great time to start taking better care of yourself. Get to the gym or start jogging a few miles every day. Start paying attention to what you eat. Meditate. Go see a personal counsellor and start developing some real solutions for tackling this bullying problem. You may not be training for the final showdown with the villain, but you're still training, and that's what's important right now.

Now that you've gotten some R & R and some new healthy habits, it's time to get to work and fix that bullying problem.

Step 2: How to Prepare for Taking a Stand

For the next month, carry a journal with you to work every day. You're going to use this journal to document instances of bullying. Fill it with dates, descriptions of events, and names of those who witnessed the events described. You're also going to offer up very short, simple, and clear gestures of resistance. The approach recommended in this book is a long play. You're going to have to be patient and do everything you can to genuinely *not care* about the behavior of the person who wants to torment you. We are emotional beings, so this won't be easy, but if you follow these steps you should steadily gain more confidence, satisfaction, and control over the situation, and in the end you'll rid yourself completely of your bullying problem.

Good bosses (who work for good companies) appreciate calm and rational approaches to solving problems. You don't want to run to your boss or HR Rep immediately after a bad encounter with your bully, head in your hands, sobbing, trembling with tears streaming down your face, demanding some immediate remediation. Emotional expression is fine, even healthy, but there's a time and a place for it. When you take your bully to task, you want to be ready for a calm, fact-based discussion with two opposing viewpoints being expressed and considered. This is the end-game you need to prepare for. So, before you get into the thick of the he-said-she-said melee, you need to make sure that you'll be going in well-armed. You become well-armed by being calm, collected, and calculated at every turn.

Don't show anyone your journal, and by all means make sure no one finds it by mistake, but do keep it close at hand. The next time your bully screams at you or makes a degrading comment, tell him/her "Don't talk to me that way," and immediately move on to addressing any relevant business matters at-hand. If there's nothing left to discuss, say something to the effect of "please leave and let me get back to work." And yes, this also applies if it's your supervisor or boss who's doing the bullying. If you are met with even further harassment (on account of your standing up for yourself), either ignore it, or repeat yourself again without getting emotional. "Don't talk to me like that." Cool and calm. ALWAYS record the details of the interaction in your journal, along with the date and the names of any witnesses present. DO NOT get angry or get into an emotional altercation of any kind. This approach is only going to work if you retain the moral high ground by keeping your end of the interaction 100% simple, clear and professional.

Other ways to lay down limits is to use your body language. If you're being shouted at and degraded, hold your hand up as if you were stopping traffic at an intersection and say "Stop." If someone gets too close to you with their body, or puts their face too close to yours, take a step back, and again, hold out your arm and say "Stop." Document the incident.

For some workplace bullying situations, these forms of simple resistance and setting of limits will suffice to put an end to the unwanted behavior. Remember, when you resist, you're not asking, you're telling, forcing the bully to either adjust their attitude or deliberately press on with inappropriate behavior after their target (you) has made it clear that you don't intend to put up with it. Unfortunately though, in many situations, simple resistance will not be enough. This is why you must meticulously document every incident in your journal (in preparation for Step 3).

One of the most important parts of your documentation will be taking note of all the witnesses present during any given incident. If a person's treatment of you is so bad that it makes you dread going to work, odds are you're not the only person with a beef. You don't necessarily need to tell your coworkers about your journal and the whole grand scheme, but you should try and enroll their help to some extent. If you trust one or more of your coworkers, tell them that you've been having trouble with a workplace bully. Tell them when and where it occurs and see if they can make arrangements to witness it. Be discrete of course. Don't go confiding to your bully's best workplace buddy and risk tipping him off. If a higher ranking employee or boss witnesses you being bullied, go to them and just confirm what they saw. Don't ask them to do anything. Tell them you're handling it, just try and weigh their reaction. Odds are they will have a very unfavorable opinion of the way you're being treated, but will probably not be eager to concern themselves with the matter. What this means, is that they will probably be happy to confirm your version of events when asked by HR a few weeks down the road, and that's a good thing. They may even wax proactive and try to nip the problem in the bud before it blows up in HR. Again, the better the company leadership, the better your chances of being able to solve this problem effectively and with finality. And if the leadership in your company is poor, well, you'll probably be better off going somewhere else where bullying isn't tolerated. You're going to come out on top either way. Remember that.

As a final note on this resist and document step. During your month of chronicling, don't slip on your general job detail. If possible, go above and beyond the call of duty this month. Complete your assignments early. Offer to help in areas outside your realm of responsibility (but not at the behest of your bully). You need your company to realize the magnitude of the loss they're going to take if they fail to meet the basic needs of a decent and valuable worker.

Step 3: The Importance of Tapping Available Support

You've bided your time for a month, drawing clear boundaries and recording infringements. Hopefully you're beginning to feel better about yourself, knowing you have a plan, and hopefully your physical health and self-esteem is in good shape. You've taken some time away from work and you know that there's life beyond your current job. You're ready to proceed in addressing this bullying problem in a calm and professional manner.

As you probably know, bullying can take place in many forms in many different environments and can involve a wide variety of parties. You're going to need to tailor your response to your specific scenario. Choosing whom you go to for support and how you go about asking for support will depend on certain variables.

One element that runs constant throughout most of these scenarios is the power of appealing to the greater interests of the company. Can you prove through your journal and the witnesses ready to corroborate with you, that the person who's harassing you is doing damage to the overall health of the

19

company? If you're one among several people that this person is bullying, then now's the time collaborate and swap notes. Even a few employees who dread being at work because of the actions of one person is not the hallmark of a well-run company.

Another highly compelling, though potentially destructive, point you could make is that the bully's behavior is putting the company at risk of a lawsuit. This is a delicate point to get across, because unless things have gotten so bad that you're on the verge of walking out, you don't want to be seen as threatening legal action against your employer. If possible, try to keep things as general as possible when making this point. This person is putting the company at risk. The risk of legal liability is especially problematic for larger companies, or those with deeper pockets, and the risk will be particularly grave if the bullying has any sexual, racial, or ageist connotation to it.

If you've got a compelling reason why the person bullying you is ultimately bad for business, and you're ready to articulate that claim in a calm, non-emotional manner, then you will probably get the best results by approaching a member or members of executive leadership rather than HR. Executive leadership staff is more likely to be concerned about the company's bottom line and if someone's behavior is getting in the way of that, there's a good chance they'll take action. Don't suggest a specific action step that you feel your superior should take. IE Don't say that you demand the company to fire the aggressor. That probably won't happen and despite how unacceptable bullying is, telling your boss to fire someone is inappropriate. Let your boss discern a response that makes sense from her own perspective.

When it comes to selecting parties in whom to confide, if the person bullying you is a coworker, then you may want to confide with your direct supervisor. If the person is your supervisor, then you may want confide with a member of higher management. If you don't think that you have a strong enough case to make – that your bully's behavior is bad for business – then you will probably want to go to HR.

If you do end up going to your company's HR department, then expect things to be done by the book and that will perhaps be slower than you'd prefer. It will be especially critical that you have thorough documentation on the encounters you've had with the bully. HR will probably want to get copies of your journal entries and will probably interview your witnesses. Afterwards they will speak to the person who is bullying you, possibly bringing you both in for a meeting at the same time. Don't get flustered when your bully starts denying and reshaping every incident you so carefully laid out in your journal. This is how bullies operate, winging it by the seat of their pants and using their bluster to intimidate everyone in their path. This is also how they inevitably falter. All you have to do is keep calm and when it's your turn to speak, be as factual and time-specific as possible, provide a very unemotional, straightforward account of what was done and said. Clearly and calmly state that you refuse to be made to work in an environment where that kind of behavior is tolerated.

Request that the events for which you have witnesses not be disclosed, at least not at first. If your bully follows her typical path of bluster and shooting from the hip she's bound to make a few mistakes and her recounting of events will not stand up to the best available evidence and witness accounts at-hand. Again, to emphasize, it's important that you proceed with calm, clarity, and with the evidence on your side. To help you prepare, practice what you're going to say beforehand. Be as concise and eloquent as you can while still getting across all the important details.

Depending on the circumstances, you may fare best by confronting the bully directly about his (or her) behavior and letting it be known that you've accumulated a month's worth of witness-verified history that could be damaging. This direct confrontation approach may be the better choice if your bully is already in a vulnerable position, perhaps from a performance standpoint. He may find it a much more expedient choice to permanently alter his behavior rather than risk another strike on his employment record.

As was stated previously, if you're a person who's secure in your ability to find another job and you're truly ready to walk out if you don't get your needs met, then you're more likely to be successful diffusing the bully problem. This is especially true if your job is one that's difficult to replace and essential to the company. If you've got a group of people together who are being bullied by the same person, then the possibility of all of you quitting will certainly weigh heavily on the company's leadership or HR team.

Whatever the result of your meeting with higher level management or HR, request that they provide some sort of signed form that documents your complaint and the action steps that are to be taken to deal with it. Make sure to hold onto this document. You may need it in Step 5.

Step 4: Pursuing Direct and Indirect Action Responses

A lot of things can happen after your first attempt at putting an end to a hostile work environment situation. The bullying may end permanently. It may end temporarily. And it may continue on as it did before without any noticeable change. If you're not ready to call it a day and move on to another job, then you may have to keep up the fight for a little while. And you do this by using Direct and Indirect Action Responses.

One Direct Action response was discussed in Step 2, where you simply tell whoever's bullying you to stop, hold your hand up like a traffic guard etc. If you've tried being calm, rational, and clear, and you've already discussed your problem with a higher ranking supervisor and/or HR, and they've yet to bring the situation under control, then you may have to add more Direct Action responses.

For example, if you're being bullied by a co-worker who is trying to get you to do more than your fair share of the workload, tell them flat out that you're not going to do any more than x amount of work. Then follow through and accept whatever fallout transpires. You can and should do the same if your supervisor is overloading you with a disproportionate or unreasonable workload. It may feel strange to deliberately ignore the orders of your supervisor, but by this point you've already pursued mediation through the proper channels. If your supervisor gets angry with you and attempts to discipline you, it will likely force another meeting with HR or higher level management, forcing the company to again confront the reality that you're being bullied by your boss. So long as the work you're doing is in reasonable to good quantity and quality, your boss will not likely want to go before his superiors and have to explain why he's piling an unreasonable workload onto you.

If you're being purposefully excluded from meetings that concern your job detail, find out when and where the meetings are being held and show up anyways. If purposeful exclusion was one of the issues you cited when having your talk with upper management or HR, then it's only expected that you're going to participate in meetings that concern your job responsibilities, even if you weren't invited.

Given that bullying detracts from the overall health of the company, focusing your Direct Action Responses in such a way that they end up benefiting the company will ultimately play out in your favor.

An example of an Indirect Action Response would be enrolling the help of a co-worker whom you're friendly with and is also a friend of the person who's bullying you. Again, you don't want to ask for help when you're upset, but when you're clear-headed. Explain that you've taken every course of action available to you including direct confrontation and you're still unable to get this person to stop harassing you. They may be able to present your plea in a way that creates a positive result.

You may also want to contact another member of the higher executive team if your first contact did not bring about results. Most companies have an Open Door policy which entitles you to reach out to anyone you please. If you do choose this Indirect Action Response path, it is best to do so subtly and discretely. Whomever you spoke with initially about the hostile work environment will likely take offense to your reaching out to someone else, especially someone higher up in the ranks.

When making contact with someone way up the ladder, like your boss' boss' boss for instance, it may be best to initiate the contact by asking for discrete advice on a work related situation. You may be surprised at how willing they'll be to set up a meeting.

Many times, higher level bosses are eager to talk with someone who can give them a frank accounting of ground-level reality. And by framing your contact as a "request for advice," you'll reduce the pressure level. When you get your meeting simply explain what you've already explained previously to HR or to other members of the executive leadership team. Share the documentation and witness collaborations you've organized in an effort to end the bullying problem. Explain what other Indirect and Direct Action Steps you've taken to deal with the problem, then listen to what your contact has to say. She may want to take action on her own volition, or she may have some ideas for you as you go forward. Remember, as always, be concise (yet detailed), calm and professional.

Step 5: How to Reassess and Chart the Next Course

You should have some clear standards in mind about what needs to be accomplished in order for you to feel comfortable, welcome, and respected at work. Has it been over a month since you've been yelled at, or been the brunt of a degrading comment? Has your workload gotten more reasonable? Are you now being included in meetings that are relevant to your work assignments? Are you no longer feeling harassed or belittled? Are you confident that this change is permanent or will you need to maintain and safeguard it? IE, was the person bullying you fired or transferred, or do you still have to see them on a regular basis?

If you're satisfied that your efforts have resulted in positive and stable change, then you should first congratulate yourself and thank those who helped you tackle and overcome a significant challenge. Secondly, you should take an inventory of your health. If you've been dealing with a bully for a prolonged amount of time, then you should arrange an appointment with your physician for a check-up. Meanwhile, get plenty of rest, exercise, and good food. Ideally, if you can, take some more time off from work (just like you did when you first initiated your anti-bullying plan).

Depending on how your situation played out, your employer/supervisors may be very much willing to give you some extra time off. After all, you've just presented them with a journal full of abuses you've suffered at work. A little bit of extra paid vacation time would probably do you good. Relax and focus on feeling good for a while. You deserve it! When you return to work, you'll be nice and refreshed and ready to direct all of your energies and focus into your job.

Rather than just return to your ordinary work-a-day life now that you're free from bullying, take your positive momentum and push forward with it. Now that this weight is off your shoulders, spend some more time doing things outside of work that you love to do. Go out to a play or movie. Take up duck hunting. Start a profile on an online dating sight and start going on a date every week. Devoting yourself to positive activities will help you heal faster and come out better for it all in the end.

If you're still feeling traumatized and saddened by what you went through, seek out some professional help. There's nothing wrong with using therapy or medication to help bring you back to state of wellness.

If the bullying situation <u>does not</u> desist, and you're still feeling that, after all your efforts, you remain bound to a hostile work environment, then it's time to make some tough choices. You don't necessarily need to leave—though you should always be willing to leave if it's your only option—but maybe you could arrange for a transfer to a different location. Maybe you could arrange to work from home? Maybe the bullying is toned down just enough thanks to your efforts that you can push through the workday while you search for a job with another company in your industry. Assess what you need in order to feel ok at work, and if you're not confident that you're going to get what you need, then figure out how to move on.

If the bullying continues and there are no options that seem reasonable to you, then maybe it's time to consult a lawyer. You've already documented at least one month's worth of bullying, and if you had some sit-downs with HR or higher-ups then you've likely received some sort of documentation from the company showing that these meetings were held and the actions the company committed for the purpose of dealing with the situation.

You usually want to avoid legal action if possible, because it will end up being expensive and there's no guarantee of success. But if, for instance, you've worked with your current company for most of your career, and you feel that finding work elsewhere will prove a near impossible feat, then you shouldn't have to stand by and suck it up just because someone showed up one day up and started making your life miserable at work.

Regardless of whether the problem was solved or lingers on, you should consider the benefits of changing work environments. Maybe this is a good time to request a transfer or to learn a new skill. If the bullying problem was severe, it may tarnish your present work environment even after the bullying itself has ended.

Conclusion

The phenomenon of bullying is widespread. Though the vast majority of working professionals condemn bullying in the workplace, it remains a misfortune that many will have to deal with at some point in their careers.

Experts agree that the root cause of bullying, workplace or otherwise, is the perpetuating party's own feelings of inadequacy. Those who engage in bullying are harboring personal psychological distress, particularly in matters of confidence and control. A great example of how this translates into the workplace is the jealous co-worker who fears that someone else may be threatening his job security, so he resorts to bullying in an effort to erode the confidence and wellbeing of the person he's threatened by.

Recent years have brought more focused awareness to the general problem and impacts of bullying. The unprecedented and confounding problem of cyberbullying has created several somber twenty-first century headlines. Film and television have brazenly tackled the subject. Thanks to this new-found awareness, employees who seek out help for a hostile work environment/bullying issue are less likely to be dismissed. Furthermore, the majority of business proprietors, supervisors, executives and board members have come to see bullying as toxic to workplace culture, capable of suppressing good talent while allowing manipulative creeps to corrupt an office or enterprise from the inside out.

Following the steps outlined in this book will likely produce a resolution or at least an improvement to your situation if you're the victim of bullying. But given the volatile and emotional nature of this type of problem, it may prove difficult to summon the patience necessary to proceed in a calm and tactical manner, as this book prescribes. The action steps in this book are meant to help you work with the options you have and ultimately win in the end, reclaiming your right to a tranquil and welcoming work environment.

Finally, I'd like to thank you for purchasing this book! If you found it helpful, I'd greatly appreciate it if you'd take a moment to leave a review on Amazon. Thank you!

Made in the USA
Lexington, KY
30 August 2016